# Do Animals Work Together?

Faith Hickman Brynie

I Like READING About ANIMALS!

# Contents

Words to Know.............. 3

Introduction............ 5

Orangutan................ 6

Hippopotamus............ 9

Bearded Dragon.......... 10

Frigate Bird............ 13

Tiger................... 14

Polar Bear............ 17

Meerkat................. 18

Bottlenose Dolphin...... 21

Weaver Ant.............. 22

Gray Wolf............... 25

Goby and Shrimp......... 26

Honeybee................ 29

Learn More

Books .............. 30

Web Sites........... 30

Index ................. 31

**Note to Parents and Teachers:** The *I Like Reading About Animals!* series supports the National Science Education Standards for K–4 science. The Words to Know section introduces subject-specific vocabulary words for the two different reading levels presented in this book (new reader and fluent reader), including pronunciation and definitions. Early readers may need help with these new words.

# Words to Know

## New Readers

**guard** (GARD)—To watch for danger.

**hive** (HYV)—The place where bees live.

**pouch** (POWCH)—A body part that looks like a bag or pocket.

## Fluent Readers

**bellow**—A deep, roaring sound.

**colony**—A group of animals of the same kind that live in the same place.

**communicate**—To share information; to make something known.

**pack**—A group of animals of the same kind that live and work together.

**predator**—An animal that eats other animals.

**territory**—The area of land where an animal lives and finds food.

# Introduction

Animals do not talk. They have other ways to tell each other what they want. They make sounds. They move in special ways. They touch each other.

## Why do animals communicate?

Animals communicate for many reasons. One reason is teamwork. Their communication helps them work together. Many animals use teamwork to survive.

Fish in groups, called schools, are safer than a fish by itself. They can escape a predator more easily than a fish alone. Some animals, such as pelicans, work together to hunt or find food. In this book, you'll discover some of the amazing ways that animals communicate and work together.

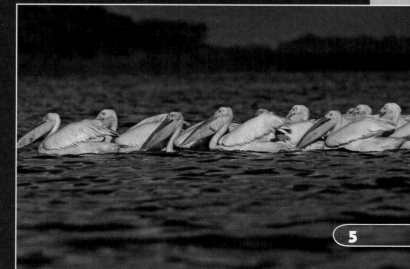

# What are these animals doing?

This is a mother orangutan. Her baby is next to her. She is kissing her baby. The kiss shows that she cares. ▷

## How do mother and baby orangutans communicate?

Orangutans live in trees. During the day, they swing from the branches. At night, they build a nest of leaves in the trees and sleep there.

Baby orangutans cling to their mothers for the first two years of their lives. The kiss shows that they are family. Staying close to its mother keeps the baby safe.

# How does a hippo use sounds?

A hippo can make sounds under the water. People do not hear these sounds. Other hippos can. The sounds mean, "Here I am. Stay away."

## Why does a hippopotamus make sounds out of the water?

Out of the water, a male hippo can let out a bellow as loud as thunder. The sound brings other hippos to the water's surface. Then they bellow, too. The sound can be heard as far as a mile (1.6 kilometers) away. The noise keeps the animals from fighting over territory. Knowing each other's locations, they keep away from each other.

9

# What is this lizard doing?

This lizard is called a bearded dragon. It opens its mouth. It raises its head. This means, "Stay away from me." ▶

## How do lizards use their bodies to communicate?

When a bearded lizard opens its mouth and raises its head, it looks strong and mean. Predators turn away from a fight. They look for other food. Other lizards stay away too. They leave the lizard alone in its territory.

When the danger goes away, the lizard settles down to soak up the sun.

# What is this bird doing?

This is a male frigate (FRIH git) bird. It can blow up the red **pouch** on its neck. Females see the red pouch. They come to the male.

## What does the frigate bird's pouch communicate?

Male frigate birds have a red pouch. Females do not. The male puffs up its red pouch, spreads its wings, and shakes its head to attract a female.

This communication gets the male and female frigate birds together. The female lays one egg on a nest in the bushes. Both parents keep the egg warm for nearly two months. Both parents care for the chick after it hatches from the egg.

# What is this tiger doing?

This tiger rubs her face on a tree. She leaves her smell on the tree. Her smell says, "Stay away from my hunting place."

14

## How can scent leave a message?

Tigers hunt alone, usually at night. They hunt deer and other large animals for food. A tiger rubs or claws a tree to leave its scent. The smell marks its territory. A tiger's territory covers many miles. A mother tiger will travel long distances in her territory to find food for herself and her cubs. Tigers sometimes defend their territories against other tigers.

# What are these polar bears doing?

One of these bears killed a seal. The other wants the seal for food. Each bear raises its head and makes noise. The bears may fight. One bear will win the food. One will run away.

## Why do polar bears fight?

Polar bears live alone most of the time. They hunt seals in the water and near the edges of the ice. Sometimes one polar bear tries to take the seal that another bear has killed. The bears stand on their back legs and push each other to show that they want the food.

A mother polar bear may fight to protect her cubs against a male. Male polar bears also fight when they are looking for a mate. Bigger, older bears usually win the fight.

# What are these meerkats doing?

Meerkats live in groups. They take turns standing **guard**. When danger comes, a meerkat barks. The others run away and hide. ▷

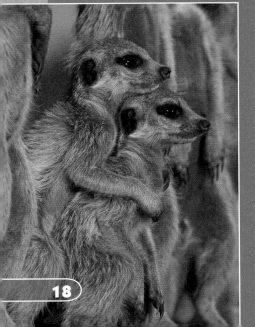

## How does teamwork keep meerkats safe?

Meerkats live in packs of as many as thirty animals. Meerkats in the same pack do not usually fight, but they may fight with meerkats from other packs. Meerkats take turns keeping watch. When a hawk or an eagle nears, the guards bark to warn the pack that danger is coming. The meerkats run for their burrows. If they cannot run away, they stand together to defend one another.

# What are these dolphins doing?

Bottlenose dolphins splash the water. They race through the water. They chase small fish toward the land. Then they can all eat the fish.

## What is strand feeding?

Bottlenose dolphins live in warm, shallow waters near shore. They eat squid, shrimp, eels, and fish. They often hunt as a pack. They swim fast through the water and drive the fish ahead of them. They chase the fish onto the muddy shores of bays and lagoons. Then they come out of the water and onto land to eat the fish. This is teamwork. They work together to trap a dinner they all can share.

# What are these ants doing?

Weaver ants build nests. They make their nests from leaves. They work as a team. They pull the leaves together. They join the leaves with silk they make.

▶

## How do weaver ants work together?

Weaver ants live and work together in large groups called colonies. One colony may contain a million ants. Some of the colony's worker ants take care of the eggs and the young ants. Other workers build nests, find food, and defend the colony. The worker ants in this picture are attacking a large beetle that has come too close to their nest.

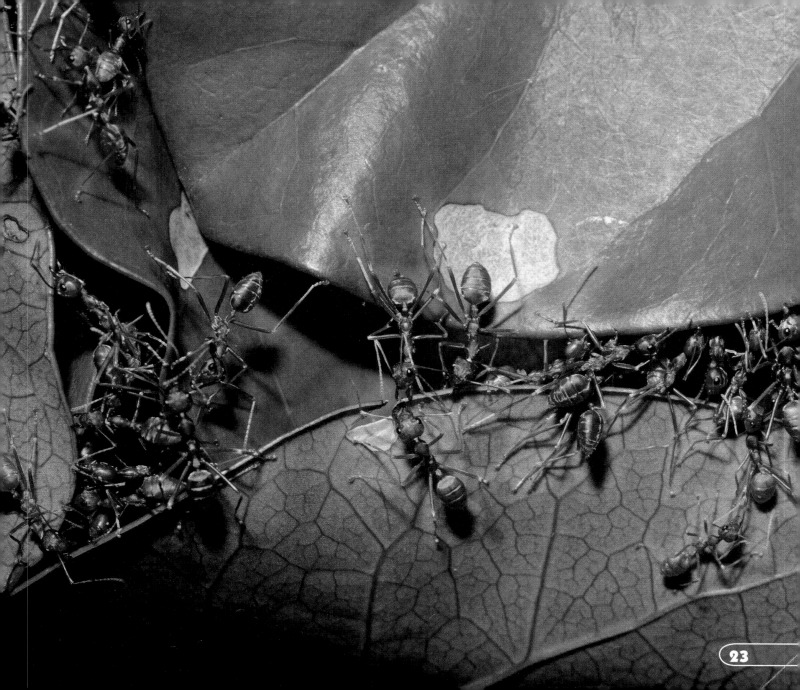

# What is this wolf doing?

◀ This gray wolf is lost from its pack. It howls.
The sound goes far. Other wolves hear the sound.
They answer. The lost wolf finds its pack.

## Why do wolves howl?

Wolves work together in packs to hunt for food. They help each other feed and care for young wolves.

Wolves know each other by their howls. They howl together to strengthen their bonds as a group. Sometimes when they howl, they wag their tails and touch each other. Wolves also bark, growl, and whimper to communicate with others in the pack.

# What are these fish doing?

The yellow fish are called gobies. They each live with a shrimp in a hole. The goby and shrimp make a good team. The shrimp digs the hole and keeps it clean. The goby guards the hole. Both kinds of animals stay safe.

## How do gobies and shrimp work as a team?

Shrimp are blind, so they cannot see danger coming. They can, however, dig burrows in which to hide. Gobies have sharp eyes. They can see predators that might eat them and the shrimp. Gobies move into the burrows the shrimp dig and act as lookouts. Both kinds of sea animals benefit from their teamwork. The goby gets a home. The shrimp gets a guard to warn it when a predator threatens.

# What are these honeybees doing?

A honeybee comes back to the **hive**. She has found food. The food is far away. She dances. The dance tells other bees where the food is.

## How do honeybees work as a team?

Most honeybees are worker bees. They travel far from the hive looking for pollen and nectar. When a worker bee finds food, she returns to the hive. She dances a "waggle dance" on the honeycomb. She twists her body from side to side as she moves up in a straight line. Then she circles back and waggles again. The dance tells other bees where to go to find the food.

This honeybee has found a flower with pollen.

29

# Learn More

## Books

Harris, Caroline. *Whales and Dolphins*. Boston: Kingfisher: 2005.

Havard, Christian. *The Wolf: Night Howler*. Watertown, Mass.: Charlesbridge, 2006.

Kaner, Etta. *Animal Talk: How Animals Communicate Through Sight, Sound and Smell*. Toronto, Ontario: Kids Can Press, 2002.

Preszler, June. *Why Do Birds Sing?: A Book About Animal Communication*. Minneapolis: First Facts, 2007.

Tatham, Betty. *How Animals Communicate*. New York: Scholastic, 2004.

## Web Sites

National Geographic Kids. *Amazing Animals*.
http://kids.nationalgeographic.com/Animals.

Wildlife Conservation Society. *Kids Go Wild*. "Wild Animal Facts."
http://kidsgowild.com/animalfacts

Yahoo Kids. *Kids Study Animals*.
http://kids.yahoo.com/animals

# Index

**A**

animal sounds, 5, 9, 17, 18, 25

**B**

baby animals, 6, 13
bearded dragon, 10
bottlenose dolphin, 21
burrow, 18, 26

**C**

chick, 13
colony, 22
communicate, 5, 6, 10, 13,
　　25, 29
cub, 14, 17

**E**

egg, 13, 22

**F**

father, 13
fight, 14, 17, 18
fish, 5, 21
food, 5, 14, 17, 21, 22, 25, 29
frigate bird, 13

**G**

goby fish, 26
gray wolf, 25
guard, 18, 26

**H**

hippopotamus, 9
hive, 29
honeybee, 29
howl, 25
hunting, 5, 14, 17, 21, 25

**L**

leaves, 6, 22
lizard, 10

**M**

meerkat, 18
mother, 6, 14, 17

**N**

nectar, 29
nest, 6, 13, 22

**O**

orangutan, 6

**P**

pack, 18, 21, 25
pelican, 5
polar bear, 17
pollen, 29
pouch, 13
predator, 5, 10, 18, 26

**S**

scent, 14
school of fish, 5
seal, 17
shrimp, 21, 26
stay away, 9, 10, 14

**T**

teamwork, 5, 18, 21, 22, 25,
　　26, 29
territory, 9, 10, 14
tiger, 14

**W**

"waggle dance," 29
weaver ant, 22

♻ Enslow Publishers, Inc., is committed to printing our book
recycled paper. The paper in every book contains 10% to 30%
consumer waste (PCW). The cover board on the outside of eac
book contains 100% PCW. Our goal is to do our part to help y
people and the environment too!

**Photo Credits: Photos by naturepl.com:** © Anup Shah, pp.
8, 9, 15; © Ben Osborne, p. 4; © Eric Baccega, pp. 16, 17;
© Francois Savigny, p. 14; © Georgette Douwma, pp. 26, 27;
© Kim Taylor, p. 28; © Lynn M. Stone, p. 25; © Marguerite S.
Van Oyen, pp. 1, 19; © Mary McDonald, pp. 10, 11; © Meul/A
p. 29; © Mike Read, p. 5; © Neil Lucas, p. 32; © Pete Oxford,
pp. 12, 13; © PREMAPHOTOS, pp. 22, 23; © Simon King, p.
© Todd Pusser, pp. 20, 21; © Tom Vezo, p. 24. **Photo by
Shutterstock:** pp. 2–3, 30–31.

**Cover Photo:** © Marguerite Smits Van Oyen/naturepl.com

**Series Science Consultant:**
**Helen Hess, PhD**
Professor of Biology
College of the Atlantic
Bar Harbor, ME

**Series Literacy Consultant:**
**Allan A. De Fina, PhD**
Dean, College of Education/Professor of Literacy Education
New Jersey City University
Past President of the New Jersey Reading Association

Enslow Elementary, an imprint of Enslow Publishers, Inc.

Enslow Elementary® is a registered trademark of Enslow Publishers, Inc.

Copyright © 2010 by Enslow Publishers, Inc.

**Library of Congress Cataloging-in-Publication Data**

Brynie, Faith Hickman, 1946–

    Do animals work together? / Faith Hickman Brynie.

      p. cm. — (I like reading about animals!)

    Includes bibliographical references and index.

    Summary: "Leveled reader that explains how different animals
work together and communicate with each other in both first
grade text and third grade text"—Provided by publisher.

    ISBN 978-0-7660-3328-3

  1. Social behavior in animals—Juvenile literature. 2. Animal
communication—Juvenile literature. I. Title.

    QL775.B79 2010

    591.5—dc22

                2008050054

ISBN-13: 978-0-7660-3749-6 (paperback ed.)

Printed in the United States of America

112009 Lake Book Manufacturing, Inc., Melrose Park, IL

10 9 8 7 6 5 4 3 2 1

**To Our Readers:** We have done our best to make sure all Internet
addresses in this book were active and appropriate when we went to
press. However, the author and the publisher have no control over
and assume no liability for the material available on those Internet
sites or on other Web sites they may link to. Any comments or sug-
gestions can be sent by e-mail to comments@enslow.com or to the
address on the back cover.

**Enslow Elementary**
an imprint of

**Enslow Publishers, Inc.**
40 Industrial Road
Box 398
Berkeley Heights, NJ 07922
USA
http://www.enslow.com

# MOLLY and the STRAWBERRY DAY

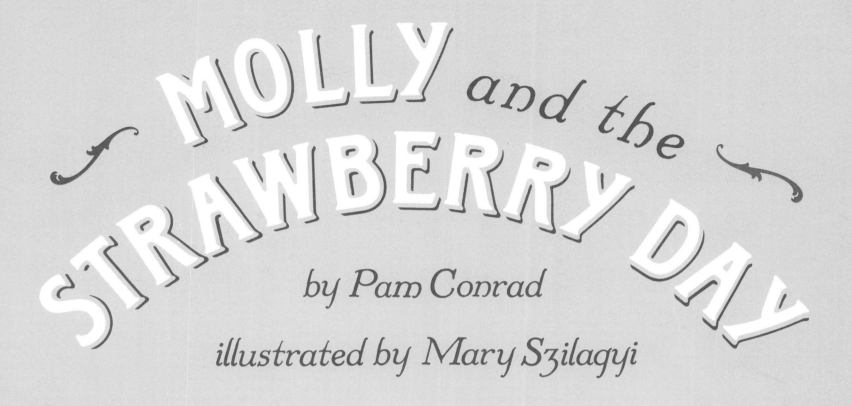

# MOLLY and the STRAWBERRY DAY

by Pam Conrad

illustrated by Mary Szilagyi

A Laura Geringer Book

An Imprint of HarperCollins Publishers

Library of Congress Cataloging-in-Publication Data
Conrad, Pam.
  Molly and the strawberry day / by Pam Conrad ; illustrated by Mary Szilagyi.
    p.      cm.
    "A Laura Geringer book."
  Summary: After a morning of strawberry-picking with her mother and father,
Molly spends her day finding new ways to enjoy her favorite fruit.
    ISBN 0-06-021369-8. – ISBN 0-06-021370-1 (lib. bdg.)
    [1. Strawberries–Fiction.]   I. Szilagyi, Mary, ill.   II. Title.   ʼ
PZ7.C76476Mo   1994                                              90-4402
[E]–dc20                                                          CIP
                                                                  AC

Typography by Christine Kettner
1   2   3   4   5   6   7   8   9   10
❖
First Edition

For Masami
–P. C.

To Alison
–M. S.

Molly loved strawberries. So early one morning, when it was strawberry-time, her mother and father took her to the strawberry fields to go picking. Molly's father had a big basket. Her mother had a medium-sized basket, and Molly had a nice little one. They stood looking out over the misty fields, and Molly's father said, "Soon we will have strawberries coming out of our ears."

Her mother set her basket on the ground and said, "Take your time, now. Pick only the bright red strawberries. Don't pick the ones that are light red or the ones that are too soft."

Her father shaded his eyes with his hand and said, "Look at the birds eating breakfast."

Molly set to work. Every time she found a nice big strawberry, she would show it to her mother. "Look, Mommy," she would say. "Look at this one!"

She offered one to her father, and he ate it right out of her hand in one loud gulp. Then he sang a song about strawberry fields.

Molly began eating the strawberries as she picked them. Molly's father stood and rubbed his stiff knees. "I'm tired already. There are too many strawberries for me. Just think, soon we will have strawberries coming out of our ears."

When the three baskets were full of strawberries, the big one, the medium-sized one, and the little one, Molly's father paid the farmer at the gate. The farmer reached down and picked up Molly to weigh her. "You ate one hundred and sixty-three strawberries, young lady. You owe me an extra two cents." Molly gave him the two pennies she had in her pocket, and they said good-bye.

As they were walking back to the car, Molly said, "I don't think I ate that many."

Molly's mother gave her a handful of strawberries to eat on the way home. She ate them carefully, saving the little green flowery stems. When they got home, Molly's father fixed a breakfast of cornflakes and strawberries for everyone. It was delicious.

Then Molly helped her mother make strawberry jelly and jam in squeaky, sparkling jars. Molly screwed the lids on tight. She stood them in a straight line. She washed her sticky hands.

For lunch she had a baloney-and-strawberry sandwich.

After lunch Molly went to her room for a nap. She dreamed about strawberries.

That afternoon Molly took the biggest, most beautiful strawberries and put them around the living room in places where everyone could admire them. She put them under the lamps, where they glistened. She put them on windowsills, where the sun shone on them. She put one on every cushion and three on the TV.

For dinner Molly's mother made spaghetti and strawberry balls, and for dessert they each had a bowl of strawberries with cream. When her father finished eating, he turned to Molly and asked, "Do you have strawberries coming out of your ears yet?" Molly smiled.

Soon the sun was setting, and the kitchen glowed pink. Molly's mother made everyone some cool strawberry tea. Then she made a strawberry facial for herself, and Molly watched her smooth it all over her face.

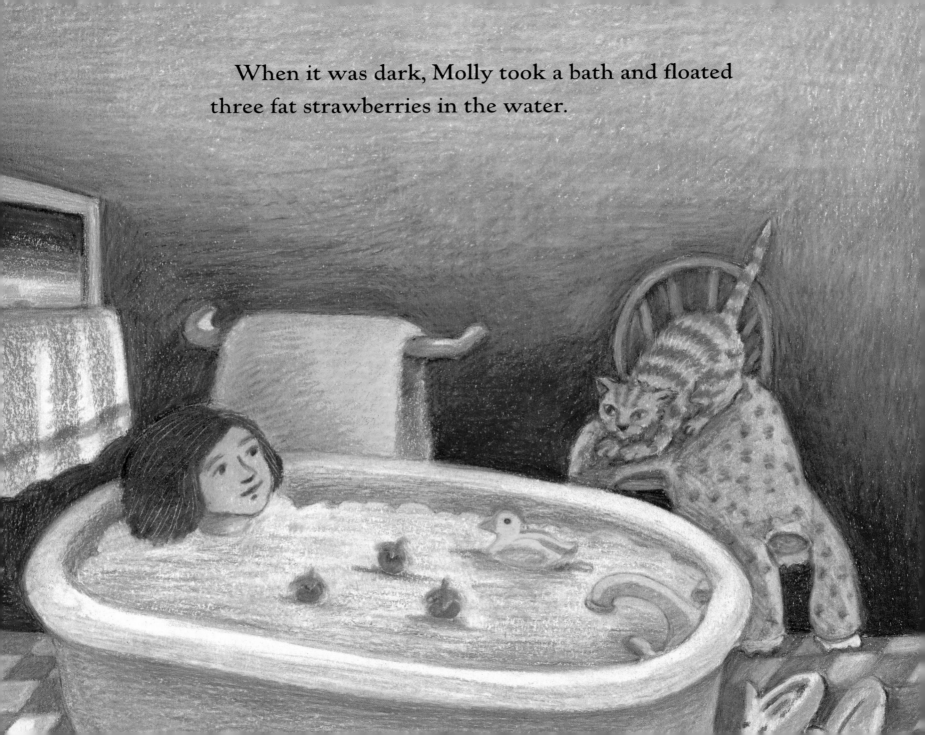

When it was dark, Molly took a bath and floated
three fat strawberries in the water.

Then she put on her nighties, the ones with the little strawberries all over, and she tried to count the strawberries on her sleeve.

And then, very, very carefully, Molly put a
strawberry in each ear . . .

and went to kiss her mother and father good night.